QUIZ # 18180

Spain : bridge between
   continents
Reading Level: 8.6. 6.7
Point Value: 2.0. 1.0

ACCELERATED READER

SPAIN

Bridge between Continents

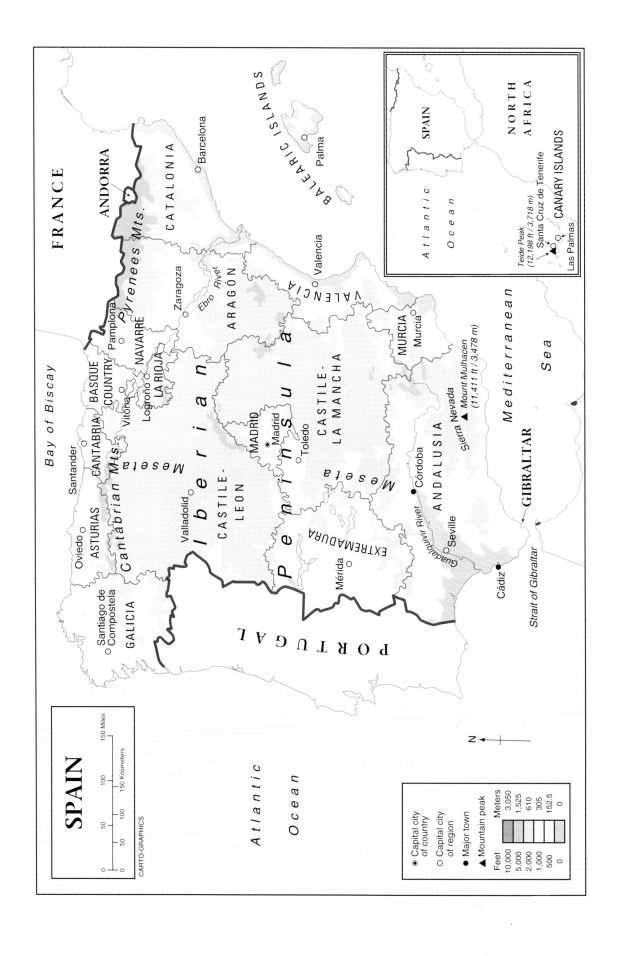

SPAIN

CARTO-GRAPHICS

Scale:
0 — 50 — 100 — 150 Miles
0 — 50 — 100 — 150 Kilometers

FRANCE

ANDORRA

Pyrenees Mts.

CATALONIA

Barcelona

BALEARIC ISLANDS

Palma

Bay of Biscay

Santander

Pamplona

Zaragoza

Ebro River

Valencia

VALENCIA

NAVARRE

BASQUE COUNTRY

Vitoria

Logroño

LA RIOJA

CANTABRIA

Cantabrian Mts.

Oviedo

ASTURIAS

Iberian

Meseta

ARAGÓN

MADRID

Madrid

Toledo

CASTILE-LA MANCHA

MURCIA

Murcia

Mediterranean Sea

Peninsula

Meseta

Sierra Nevada

Mount Mulhacén
(11,411 ft / 3,478 m)

ANDALUSIA

Córdoba

Guadalquivir River

Seville

GIBRALTAR

Cádiz

Strait of Gibraltar

CASTILE-LEON

Valladolid

EXTREMADURA

Mérida

Santiago de Compostela

GALICIA

PORTUGAL

Atlantic Ocean

N

SPAIN

NORTH AFRICA

Atlantic Ocean

Teide Peak
(12,198 ft / 3,718 m)

Santa Cruz de Tenerife

CANARY ISLANDS

Las Palmas

Legend:
- ◉ Capital city of country
- ○ Capital city of region
- ● Major town
- ▲ Mountain peak

Feet	Meters
10,000	3,050
5,000	1,525
2,000	610
1,000	305
500	152.5
0	0

SPAIN

Bridge between Continents

Stephen Chicoine

BENCHMARK BOOKS

MARSHALL CAVENDISH
NEW YORK

*With thanks to Professor Bernardo Antonio González,
Department of Romance Languages and Literatures
at Wesleyan University, for his expert review
of the manuscript.*

Benchmark Books
Marshall Cavendish Corporation
99 White Plains Road
Tarrytown, New York 10591-9001

© Marshall Cavendish Corporation 1997

Library of Congress Cataloging-in-Publication Data

Chicoine, Stephen.
    Spain: bridge between continents / by Stephen Chicoine.
        p.   cm. — (Exploring cultures of the world)
    Summary: Examines the geography, people, customs, and history of one of the largest countries on the continent of Europe.
    ISBN 0-7614-0143-1 (lib. bdg.)
    1. Spain—Juvenile literature. [1. Spain.] I. Title. II. Series.
  DP17.C45   1997
  946—dc21
                                                      96-45498
                                                       CIPxx
                                                         AC

Printed in Hong Kong

Series design by Carol Matsuyama

Front cover: Young Andalusian girl in traditional costume
Back cover: The Plaza de España in Seville

Photo Credits

Front cover: ©Steve Vidler/Leo de Wys; back cover: ©Arthur Hustwitt/Leo de Wys; title page and pages 28, 29, 30: ©Hilary Wilkes/International Stock Photo; page 6: North Wind Picture Archives; pages 9, 23, 36, 42, 46: ©Chad Ehlers/International Stock Photo; page 11: ©J.G. Edmanson/International Stock Photo; pages 14–15, 55: ©Blackbirch Inc.; page 17: ©Bridgeman/Art Resource, NY; pages 19, 56: ©Giraudon/Art Resource, NY; page 22: ©Action Press/SABA; pages 24, 41, 52: ©Paul Thompson/International Stock Photo; page 27: ©Stockman/International Stock Photo; page 32: ©Stephanie Maze/National Geographic Society; page 34: ©Joseph J. Scherschel/National Geographic Image Collection; page 35: David A. Harvey/©National Geographic Society; page 39: ©Robert Tulin/International Stock Photo; page 45: ©Robert Arakaki/International Stock Photo; page 49: ©Edwin Grosvenor/National Geographic Society; page 50: ©Tourist Office of Spain; page 51: ©Kit Luce/International Stock Photo; page 58: ©James P. Blair/National Geographic Image Collection

Contents

The great warrior El Cid was respected by the armies of both the Christians and the Muslims who battled for control of the Iberian Peninsula.

1

GEOGRAPHY AND HISTORY

Land of Beauty and Power

The Warrior El Cid

The brave Spanish knight with the long beard rode into battle on a powerful stallion. The sword he wielded had been won in combat from a great warrior. His armor was decorated with silver and gold. And on his shield was the image of a fearsome dragon.

Never defeated in battle, the knight, Rodrigo Díaz, was respected by both the Christians and the Muslim Arabs who fought for control of the Iberian Peninsula, in southwest Europe. He became known as El Cid. This name came from the Arabic word for "lord."

El Cid fought for the first time for the Christian kingdom of Castile, at the age of twenty, in the year A.D. 1063. This was a time when Christian lords were fighting against one another as well as against the Arab leaders. El Cid's fame as a warrior grew quickly, and he became a great leader in battle.

The King of Castile, Alfonso VI, soon became jealous of El Cid. King Alfonso banished the knight from his kingdom. El Cid vowed not to cut his beard until he was pardoned. He wore it very long for many years, braided and tied with a cord so that no one could grab it in battle.

Rejected by King Alfonso, El Cid served the Arab ruler of a nearby kingdom for several years. He fought both Christians and Muslims and won many battles. Later, he became a powerful lord in his own right in the region of Valencia, along the Mediterranean coast.

In 1086, the Almoravids, a people from the deserts of North Africa, entered the Iberian Peninsula. They had come at the request of Arab rulers in Iberia who were concerned about the rising power of Castile. The Almoravids immediately won a great battle against King Alfonso and his Castilians. The Christians continued to suffer one defeat after another at the hands of the Almoravids. People soon came to believe that the Almoravids were invincible.

In 1094, a vast Almoravid army laid siege to El Cid's fortress, which lay near the Muslim city of Valencia. El Cid and his warriors were greatly outnumbered. For ten days, they remained within the walls of the fortress. El Cid patiently waited for the right moment to fight. Meanwhile, the Almoravids grew more and more confident.

Then El Cid rode out, leading 4,000 knights. He carefully picked his battleground to limit the number of Almoravids that could face him at any one time. The battle was fought on the plains just east of Valencia.

El Cid and his men charged to the attack shouting "Santiago," the name of their patron saint. They drove through the enemy line. Then they wheeled around and attacked again before the Almoravids could prepare themselves. It was a great victory for El Cid.

You should have seen so many lances lowered and raised,
so many shields perforated and pierced,
so many coats of mail broken and dented,
so many white pennants held high, red with blood,
so many good horses running riderless.

– From *The Poem of The Cid*

The rich city of Valencia became the capital of El Cid's personal kingdom. He converted the city's chief mosque—the Muslim house of worship—into a Christian cathedral. Famous across Iberia, he lived out his last years amid great wealth and splendor and died peacefully in 1099. Nine centuries later, he remains the hero of the people of España, *the modern nation of Spain.*

A Bridge to Africa

Modern Spain, which takes up most of the Iberian Peninsula, is one of the largest countries on the continent of Europe. It has about the same land area as the states of Utah and Arizona combined. Mainland Spain is broken down into sixteen major regions, something like the U.S. states. These regions

Rugged mountains are a natural border in northern Spain. This village of Torla is nestled in the Pyrenees.

may contain one or more provinces, which may be compared to U.S. counties. The nation is bordered on the northeast by France and the tiny nation of Andorra. The rugged Pyrenees Mountains, which march across the neck of the Iberian Peninsula, mark these borders. On the west lies Portugal. Spain shares Iberia with this small country.

Much of Spain's border is coastline. The Mediterranean Sea laps the shores on the south and east, while the powerful Atlantic Ocean lies to the southwest and northwest. The territory of Spain also includes the Canary Islands in the Atlantic, the Balearic Islands in the Mediterranean, and a few other small places.

Because of its strategic geographic location, Iberia has been a battlefield between Europe and Africa for almost 2,000 years. Spain's southern tip is separated from the northern tip of Africa by only a narrow waterway, the Strait of Gibraltar.

A Rugged Land

The major feature of the central Iberian Peninsula is the Meseta, a high, flat area. It was on this plateau that the Christian kingdoms of Castile and Aragon developed. These kingdoms became the core of modern Spain.

The Meseta is nearly surrounded by mountain ranges, including the Cantabrian Mountains in the north and the Sierra Morena in the south. Another range, the Sierra Nevada, lies in the extreme south of Spain. With these and other ranges, plus the lofty Pyrenees in the north, it is no wonder that, among European countries, only Switzerland is more mountainous than Spain.

The highest peak on the Spanish mainland is found in the Sierra Nevadas. Mount Mulhacen rises 11,411 feet (3,478

The Canary Islands, which lie off the coast of Africa, are a part of the territory of Spain. The islands boast both lofty mountain peaks and tranquil sea harbors.

meters) into the sky. However, Teide Peak, in the Canary Islands, is the highest peak in the entire Spanish nation, soaring 12,198 feet (3,718 meters).

The rugged Spanish terrain has always made travel and communications difficult. For this reason, it took a long time to unite the different peoples of Spain into one modern nation. It also helps to explain why Spain remains a country of very distinct regions. Even today, the peoples of these regions maintain their special customs and ways of life.

Maritime to Continental

Like the people and the land, Spain's climate varies greatly. The coastal regions of eastern and southern Spain enjoy a moderate, Mediterranean climate year-round. Northern and northwestern Spain have a cooler maritime climate, lying as they do along the Atlantic coast. These regions receive the most rainfall.

The interior of Spain is dry, receiving little rain or snow. This is because its many mountain ranges block clouds that would otherwise bring rain from the Atlantic Ocean and the Mediterranean Sea. For much of the year, the Pyrenees and Cantabrian Mountains tend to keep the warm, dry air from North Africa in place over the peninsula. Summers are generally hot. The winters in the interior, however, can be bitterly cold.

Two major river systems—the Ebro and the Guadalquivir—cross the Meseta. But, while many rivers crisscross the Spanish countryside, they have low levels of water. This is especially true during the hot, dry summers. As a result, the rivers have never been very important for transporting goods and people.

The Early Iberians

Humans may have lived on the Iberian Peninsula for as long as a million years. Not much is known about the earliest Iberians. But the Celts, a people from northern Europe, are believed to have invaded Iberia in the 800s B.C. The Celts and Iberians eventually mixed to form what have been called the Celtiberians.

By 800 B.C., traders from the great Mediterranean civilizations of Phoenicia and Greece were also establishing settlements in Iberia. They settled along the Mediterranean coast. Many of Spain's major cities along the coast have their origins in these ancient times.

Hispania

In 206 B.C., armies from the Roman Empire to the east invaded Iberia. Within a century, the powerful Romans had taken control of the land and peoples of Iberia.

Roman civilization flourished on the Iberian Peninsula. The Romans called this land *Hispania* (ees-PAHN-ya). The Spanish word for Spain, *España* (es-PAHN-ya), comes from this ancient name.

Latin, the language of the ancient Romans, became the language of Iberia as well. Only the Basque people of the northern part of the peninsula refused to adopt Latin. They steadfastly kept their own language, Euskera (ay-oo-SKEH-rah). In fact, some of them still speak it today, more than 2,000 years later!

In the A.D. 300s, Christianity was officially adopted as the religion of the Roman Empire. The Iberians also gradually accepted Christianity.

The Romans' powerful influence can be seen in modern Spain in yet another way. Their carefully laid-out military settlements became the foundation for Iberia's early towns—and, later, its modern cities. The Romans supplied their towns with running water by means of aqueducts—large pipes that carried water for miles down from the mountains. The remains of these aqueducts, as well as the ruins of huge amphitheaters and public buildings, can still be seen in the Spanish countryside. Other Roman contributions include the cultivation of olives, grapes, and garlic.

The Fall of Rome

In the 300s, Germanic tribes from northern Europe began to threaten the Roman Empire. Rome fell to these invading peoples in the 400s. These tribes soon crossed the Pyrenees Mountains and invaded the Iberian Peninsula. One tribe, the Visigoths, ultimately gained control.

The Visigoths adopted Christianity, further strengthening that religion in Iberia. However, they fought among themselves, and their power in Iberia gradually weakened. In the 700s, they were defeated by a new wave of invaders, this time from the south—from North Africa.

The Kingdom of al-Andalus

In 711, an Arab army crossed the Strait of Gibraltar from North Africa into Spain. (The name *Gibraltar* comes from an Arabic phrase meaning "Rock of Tariq," referring to Tariq, the Arabs' military leader.) These Arabs were

The ancient Romans built great stone structures, called aqueducts, which carried water down from the mountains. Their remains can still be seen in modern Spain.

Muslims, followers of the Prophet Muhammad. Their religion, called Islam (ISS-lam), had spread rapidly since it was founded by Muhammad in the previous century. The Arabs quickly defeated the Visigoths and gained control of much of Iberia. Their kingdom became known as al-Andalus.

A group of Christians retreated to the Cantabrian Mountains in the north of Iberia. They started a small kingdom, called Asturias. This tiny kingdom was the first of many Christian kingdoms. Gradually, these kingdoms would unite to drive the Muslims from the peninsula.

That ultimate victory, though, was not achieved for more than 700 years. The Spanish refer to it as the *Reconquista* (ray-con-KEY-sta), or the "reconquering." It was one of the most important times in Spanish history.

A Flourishing Civilization

The Arabs of al-Andalus had a huge impact on the culture of the peninsula. Some of the world's greatest architectural treasures were built during this period. Córdoba became one of the largest and richest cities in all the world. La Mezquita, Córdoba's Great Mosque, completed in 976, mirrors that past glory. La Mezquita remains one of the largest mosques in the world. More than 800 pillars support striped marble arches in a stunning display. The arts and sciences also flourished in this period. And public institutions such as hospitals, libraries, and schools were established.

From Tolerance to the Inquisition

A family of Arab rulers known as the Umayyads (OO-my-yads) governed Iberia for 300 years, starting in the 700s. Under these Muslim rulers, all religions were tolerated, or respected. Muslims, Christians, and Jews lived peacefully alongside one another. There was still conflict in this period, though. This was the result of various warlords, both Christian and Muslim, fighting for power and wealth.

Religious tolerance ended when one Christian kingdom, Castile, became very powerful. Castile united the Christian peoples and led them into battle against the Muslims.

Religious intolerance in Spain reached its peak during the Inquisition, when courts were set up to put non-Christians on trial.

The name Castile comes from the Spanish word *castilla,* which means "castle." The region is still dotted with castles. Each was built long ago to defend territory "reconquered" from the Muslims.

By the 1200s, the Muslim hold on the Iberian Peninsula had been, for the most part, broken. However, in the 1400s, the Muslims still controlled Granada, their rich kingdom in the south.

The core of modern Spain was established in 1469 with the marriage of two Christian rulers: Ferdinand of Aragon and Isabella of Castile. Their combined kingdom was unusual in that it included many Jews and Muslims.

But in 1478, the "Catholic Monarchs," as Ferdinand and Isabella were known, because of their Roman Catholic (Christian) faith, began what became known as the Inquisition. This was a frightening and brutal time. People who were not Christians, such as Muslims and Jews, were treated as enemies of society. They were sought out, questioned, even tortured for practicing their faiths. Many were killed. Roman Catholicism became not only the official religion of Spain, but also the only religion allowed. The Inquisition did not end until the seventeenth century.

The *Reconquista* Is Completed

In 1491, the combined armies of King Ferdinand and Queen Isabella laid siege to the Muslim stronghold of Granada, to force the Muslims out of Spain. Seven months later, in January 1492, Granada surrendered to the Christians. The *Reconquista* was then complete. That same year, Ferdinand and Isabella ordered all remaining Jews who refused to become Christians to leave Spain.

A World Power

In 1492, a group of three ships left Spain, sponsored by Ferdinand and Isabella. Led by Christopher Columbus, an Italian, this sea voyage resulted in the discovery of the Americas by the Europeans.

As a result of their sponsorship of Columbus, Ferdinand and Isabella laid claim to the Americas. Spanish conquistadores (con-keys-tah-DOOR-ez), or "conquerors," soon established control over many of the peoples of the Americas. The conquistadores spread the Christian religion

In this detail of a painting, Christopher Columbus, accompanied by Indians from the Americas, greets Queen Isabella and King Ferdinand.

and established colonies. But they were really more interested in fighting and becoming rich.

In this way, Spain became the first European power to have an overseas empire. Its colonies in the Americas provided it with almost unimaginable wealth. As a result, in the early 1500s, Spain was the greatest European power, especially in the Americas. The Spanish imprint in Mexico and Central and South America remains to this day. Spanish is the language of most of the countries in that large region, for example, and the majority of the people are Roman Catholics.

SPANISH GOVERNMENT

Spain is a constitutional monarchy. This means that the head of state is a monarch (today, King Juan Carlos) who must follow the basic laws set forth in the Constitution. The king is the head of state and represents Spain in international matters. In this role, the king can sign treaties and declare war.

Spain has a parliamentary system of government. The Parliament, or *Cortes* (COR-tez), consists of two houses: the Congress of People's Deputies and the Senate. Members of each serve four-year terms.

The Congress has 350 members. They are elected by the people. The number of deputies for each of Spain's fifty provinces (forty-seven on the mainland and three in the territories) depends on each province's population.

The Senate has 256 members. Each of the forty-seven provinces on the mainland elects four senators, regardless of the size of population of the province. In 1983, the country's fifty provinces were grouped into seventeen regions. The people in each region share similar customs and history. Each region has its own capital, with its own provincial council. And each region elects at least one senator, based on population.

The prime minister, or head of government, is usually the leader of the political party that has the most deputies in Congress. The king formally appoints the prime minister and cabinet ministers, with the help of the *Cortes*.

Decline of an Empire

King Philip III established Madrid as the capital of a "united" Spain in 1606. But not all groups wanted to be part of the nation. In 1640, the people of the region of Catalonia revolted. The rebellion was put down. In that same year, however, Portugal, which had been under the Spanish crown for four decades, won its independence for good. Some regions of the country continued in large part to rule themselves.

In the 1700s and 1800s, a new family ruled Spain, the Bourbons. Under the Bourbon kings, Spain became involved in many wars for control of Europe and the Americas.

Most of Spain's colonies in the Americas declared their independence in the early 1800s. In the Spanish-American War of 1898, Spain also lost the islands of the Philippines, Puerto Rico, Guam, and Cuba. Its great colonial empire had disappeared. Spain's role as a major world power had ended.

Democracy—and Dictatorship

In the 1920s, the Spanish people began demanding a government that would respond to their needs and wants. In 1931, King Alfonso XIII stepped down from the throne, and a republic was formed. In this form of government, the power lies with the citizens, who elect the leaders.

In 1936, a group of military officers, led by General Francisco Franco, rose up to gain control of the government. A bitter struggle for power followed, known as the Spanish Civil War. Well over half a million people died in three bloody years of fighting. The Nationalists, as Franco's side was known, finally won. Franco then established a dictatorship, in which all power was concentrated in his hands.

The dictator ruled Spain with an iron fist for forty years. There were few freedoms for the people of Spain under General Franco. For example, people were not allowed freedom of speech. The content of newspapers, books, movies, and plays was strictly controlled by the government. Those who dared to speak out against the government were often thrown into prison or forced to leave the country.

Franco wanted a Spain that was united under his rule. To this end, he took away the right of Catalonia, the Basque provinces, and Galicia to govern themselves. Franco even outlawed use of the Catalan, Galician, and Basque languages.

Franco picked Juan Carlos, King Alfonso XIII's grandson, to rule Spain after his death. He wanted Spain to return to a monarchy, but he also wanted the people to remain closely controlled by the government. Franco died on November 20, 1975. Juan Carlos became king two days later.

A New Era Begins

King Juan Carlos did not follow Franco's plan, however. Instead, he introduced measures to install a true democracy in Spain—a political system that represented the people.

Today, Spain is a modern nation that contributes to the global economy. Spain is a member of the North Atlantic Treaty Organization and the European Union. There was

The royal family. From left to right, Jaime, Elena, King Juan Carlos, Queen Sophia, Felipe, and Cristina.

Spain has both a rich heritage and a promising future as part of Europe. These people are enjoying a stroll through Las Ramblas, a central meeting place in the prosperous city of Barcelona.

difficulty for some time being accepted into these important regional organizations. The towering Pyrenees Mountains have always set Spain apart from the rest of Europe. Thus, Spain has been viewed by some people in Europe as almost an "outsider." But King Juan Carlos's political changes helped to bring about Europe's acceptance of Spain.

A Unique Blend

Modern Spain reflects the influence of both European and North African cultures. Despite the efforts to eliminate the Arabs from Spain, their historical legacy can still be seen throughout the land, in its architecture, food, and language. Yet Spanish culture also reflects its contact with peoples from all over Europe. Thus, Spain stands today as it always has, as the bridge between the continents of Europe and Africa.

This young man and woman show off their traditional costumes from Galicia, a region in northern Spain.

2

THE PEOPLE

A Kaleidoscope of Peoples

The Catalans

Catalonia, located in the northeastern corner of Spain, has the largest population of any of Spain's regions. Its terrain varies from the beautiful beaches of Costa Brava (the "Brave Coast") to the rugged mountains inland.

Catalans still follow many ancient customs, as you can easily see if you visit the city of Barcelona on a Sunday. That day, people gather in the streets to dance the *sardana*. This is one of the most famous traditions of the Catalan people. In the *sardana*, big circles of dancers move slowly to the rhythm of the music.

Catalans are fiercely proud of their regional identity. They have spoken and written their own language, Catalan, for centuries. In Catalonia, street signs are written in both Spanish and Catalan.

Catalans are generally well respected as business people. In fact, many people consider Barcelona, the capital of

Catalonia, to be the commercial capital of Spain. Barcelona is an elegant and sophisticated city, with a strong artistic tradition. Its Liceu is one of the leading opera houses in Europe. In 1992, Barcelona hosted the Summer Olympic Games.

The Valencians

The region of Valencia is located south of Catalonia, down the Mediterranean Coast. It is centered around the city of the same name. Although it is itself a distinct region, the people of Valencia speak Catalan. However, in contrast to Catalonia, Valencia was greatly influenced by the Arabs.

Valencia is well known for its crafts and for its beautiful orchards—in particular, its oranges. The Arabs introduced the orange, or *naranja*, to Spain. Today, Valencians harvest the juicy fruit during much of the year.

The Basques

The Basques are perhaps the most distinctive people of Spain. Their language, Euskera, has no known ties with any other language. Its origins are unknown. Basques live on both sides of the Pyrenees Mountains, in both Spain and France. The Basques have always fought fiercely to hold on to their separate identity. Many Basque men still wear the *txapela* (chah-PEL-ah), their distinctive beret.

The Basques traditionally farmed small plots of land widely separated from one another in their mountainous region. Each homestead usually consisted of a farmhouse set on the slope of a hill with a nearby stable for cows or sheep, a pasture, and perhaps an apple orchard. The isolation of these settlements resulted in close family ties. Basque families are still very tightly knit.

The Barcelona Stock Exchange is part of the thriving economy of Catalonia.

27

The Andalusians

When people think of Spain, they often think of Andalusia as "typically Spanish." This region, in southern Spain, has hill towns whose buildings are painted a sparkling white, vast groves of olive trees, and flamenco dancing. Yet Andalusia reflects the glorious period of Arab rule more than any other region. Muslim craftsmanship is found everywhere. Windows are decorated with ornate metal grillwork, and floors and walls shimmer with beautiful blue ceramic tiles. In the

An old castle sits high above the gleaming town of Césares, in Andalusia.

The Alhambra, with its manicured gardens and intricate workmanship, is one of the most beautiful examples of Arabic architecture in Spain. The famous palace and fortress is located in Granada, a city in Andalusia.

late afternoon, people relax in beautiful gardens that were designed centuries ago.

Andalusia's woven silk and brocade fabrics, as well as its beautiful leather products, are loved throughout Europe. At church, women can often be seen wearing black mantillas (man-TEE-yas). A mantilla is a light scarf that covers the head and the shoulders. It is usually draped over a comb that is firmly anchored high on the head. White mantillas are worn for festive occasions, such as bullfights.

The Castilians

The region of Castile—the land of castles—has been the heart of Spain for many centuries. The soil in Castile is dry and barren. As a result, it has been necessary to graze livestock across broad areas. For many generations, ranchers could be seen tending to their large herds on horseback. When the

One of the many government buildings in Madrid, the nation's capital city. Madrid lies in the center of the country, in the region of Castile.

Spaniards colonized the Americas, they introduced open-range ranching there. They also brought spurs and the practice of branding, both of which come from Castile.

The People of Extremadura and Asturias

Extremadura is one of the most rural regions of Spain. Many of the people of this arid land in the west, along the Portuguese border, still tend their flocks of sheep as they have for centuries. The people are strong and hardy. Many of the conquistadores who went to the Americas long ago came from Extremadura.

The herders of mountainous Asturias, another region of Spain, also still tend livestock. They are known for their yodeling, or singing, a centuries-old way of communicating across valleys. Asturias is also known for its coal-mining and steel-manufacturing industries.

The Galicians

Yet another region is Galicia, located in the northwest corner of Spain, on the Atlantic coast. Some 3,000 years ago, the region was invaded by the Celts, the ancestors of today's Irish and Scots. Galicians are noted for their blond hair and light eyes. They still practice many Celtic traditions, such as playing the bagpipes. Today, as they have for centuries, most Galicians make their living by fishing.

Changing Ways of Life

For most of its history, Spain was a rural, agricultural country. Villagers lived in large family groups. Cousins grew up together, and grandparents helped to raise the children. Everyone worked together in the fields and around the home.

Many Spaniards rarely left their regions. This helped to keep the different regional cultures strong.

However, Spain has changed dramatically in recent years. Franco began the process of modernization. The first step was to industrialize the economy. In 1950, more than half of the jobs in Spain were in agriculture. Today, only one fifth of Spaniards work in agriculture.

As a result of industrialization, Spaniards began moving into the cities. This is the same transformation that took place in some other European countries and the United States in the early 1900s. More than three fourths of the

Family life is very important to Spaniards. Here, relatives gather outdoors for a picnic.

SAY IT IN SPANISH

Spanish is the major language of Spain. Other official languages are Catalan, Gallegos, and Euskera.

Hi! Hello!	*¡Hola!* (OH-lah)
Good-bye!	*Adios.* (ah-dee-OS)
Good morning.	*Buenos días.* (BWAY-nohs DEE-ahs)
Good afternoon.	*Buenas tardes.* (BWAY-nahs TAHR-dehs)
Good evening.	*Buenas noches.* (BWAY-nahs NOH-chehs)
What's going on?	*¿Qué pasa?* (keh PAH-sah)
My name is____.	*Me llamo____.* (may YAH-mo____)
How are you?	*¿Cómo está Usted?* (COH-mo es-TAH oo-STEHD)
I'm well.	*Estoy bien.* (ehs-TOY bee-EHN)
Thank you.	*Gracias.* (GRAH-see-us)

people of Spain now live in towns and cities. This urbanization is an important change for Spain, with many far-reaching effects on how people live and think.

Many Spanish cities have not had much time to adjust to their rapid growth. As in other industrialized countries, overcrowding, crime, and pollution are among the many challenges that urban Spaniards face. These are problems they share with many other cities of the world.

Bountiful Harvests

Although it no longer is the basis of Spain's economy, agriculture is still important. In fact, Spain sells large amounts of its crops to other countries.

Farmers produce a lot of wheat and barley. There are also many olive groves. Spain leads the world in the production of olive oil, and flavorful Spanish olives are eaten the world over. Vast stretches of olive trees cover miles of hillsides in southern Spain and along the Mediterranean coast. These ancient groves are carefully tended. To harvest olives, workers climb up a ladder and beat the branches with a stick.

In rural Andalusia, many children grow up working with their parents in the family's olive groves. Their fruit orchards also produce valuable crops. In addition, many Spaniards raise livestock, including sheep, goats, and cattle. This practice is most common in the hilly pastures of the northern parts of the country.

Wine production is also important. Spanish wines are enjoyed by people around the world.

In Andalusia, workers harvest olives by beating the trees with sticks.

These Basque women sort and pack anchovies in the harbor of Bermeo, on the Atlantic coast.

Coastal Catches

People have fished along Spain's long coastline since the beginning of time. Although not as important as in the past, fishing is still a major industry, especially in the north.

The coastline has given rise to another valuable industry: tourism. The beaches along the Mediterranean coast are among the most famous in the world. Northern Europeans visit Spain every summer to enjoy its sand and sea. People also come from around the world to marvel at Spain's beautiful towns and cities. Many love to stay at the old castles and convents that have been made into picturesque hotels.

Flowers, tossed from balconies, blanket a Corpus Christi parade in Valencia.

3

FAMILY LIFE, FESTIVALS, AND FOOD

Wonderful Food, Colorful Fiestas

The scene is the same in nearly every village, town, and city in Spain. Every evening between 8:00 and 10:00, people join in the *paseo* (pah-SAY-oh), the evening promenade. It is the major social event of the day.

The evenings in Spain are cool and pleasant. During the *paseo*, entire families stroll along the main avenue. Young men exchange smiles with young women. People sit at sidewalk cafés and watch their friends and neighbors go by. There they sip drinks and eat tasty snacks while extending greetings to passersby.

Families: Taking Time to Enjoy Life

Even though Spain has become a mainly urban country, one important thing has not changed: Among Spaniards, family ties remain strong. They take every opportunity to work and play together.

Family members gather in the morning, afternoon, and evening to enjoy one another's company over meals. Food is

FLAN: BAKED CUSTARD

4 cups milk

4 eggs, slightly beaten

1 cup sugar

1 teaspoon vanilla

1/4 teaspoon salt

pinch of nutmeg

8 custard cups

Preheat oven to 325° F. Pour milk into saucepan and add the sugar, vanilla, and salt. Stir. Simmer slowly for about 6 minutes. Let the mixture cool for a few minutes and add the eggs. Stir. Pour into custard cups.

Place filled cups in a pan of hot water. The water should cover the bottom two thirds of cups. Bake for 45 minutes or until the custard is slightly browned on top and no longer clings to a knife. Do not allow water to boil. Usually the custard will be done at about the time the water is just about to boil. If water seems about to boil when the custard is not yet baked, add cold water.

Remove the cups and chill. Be sure to ask an adult to help you remove the molds from the hot water. Sprinkle with nutmeg before serving.

Serves 8.

an important part of life in Spain. Spaniards take time to enjoy not only the meal, but also good conversation with friends and family.

Breakfast is usually a light meal. It often consists of deep-fried pastries called *churros*, and hot chocolate or coffee.

The main meal of the day generally begins no earlier than 2:00 P.M. The family gathers around the table and may linger there together until 3:00 or 4:00. It is a large meal that includes several courses, such as soup, salad, chicken or another main dish, and dessert. Afterwards, many people take a siesta, the afternoon rest or nap.

Small snacks, called *tapas*, may be eaten late in the afternoon and in the early evening. This leads naturally to the *paseo*. After the evening stroll comes yet another light meal. People may not start eating this meal until 10:00 or even 11:00 P.M.!

A Delight to Experience

The cuisine of Spain reflects the country's many different cultural traditions. One of the most famous dishes is *paella Valenciana*. This dish from Valencia is made of rice cooked in olive oil and seasoned with saffron, a fragrant, yellow spice. Valencians generally add chicken or rabbit and perhaps vegetables. Other Spanish regions have also adopted *paella* and will often add shrimp, mussels, and fish.

The natives of Toledo enjoy *codornices a la Toledana*, quail served with vegetables. In Aragon, lamb is combined with tomatoes and peppers and topped off with strips of sweet red peppers to make the delicious *chilindron*.

The Basques love to eat cod and squid. But perhaps their most remarkable dish is *al pil-pil*, eels that are flavored with garlic and red pepper. Empanadas, the delicious pastry pies of Galicia, are stuffed with shrimp, mussels, crab, and nearly anything else that comes from the sea.

Catalans, like the Galicians, eat a lot of fish. Among the many sauces that they serve over fish is *romesco*. It is made of tomatoes, garlic, onions, red peppers, and almonds mixed with olive oil. Catalans are also quite proud of their *zarzuela*, a tomato-based fish stew.

This paella *from Andalusia is a mixture of rice, seafood, and chicken, cooked with saffron.*

One Castilian specialty is *cochinillo asado*, roast suckling pig. Within Castile, the area of La Mancha—on the Meseta—is famous for its *pisto manchego*, a vegetable dish, as well as its *cocido*, a stew.

Madrid, as the nation's capital, offers a mix of the dishes of each of Spain's regions. However, the people of Madrid have their own special dishes as well. *Cocido Madrileño* is a stew consisting of sausage, bacon, ham, chicken, potatoes, and garbanzo beans. It is served in small clay pots after simmering for hours.

Fiesta!

Throughout the land and for many centuries, the Spanish people have enjoyed holding religious celebrations, or fiestas. Most Spaniards—98 percent—are Roman Catholics. Often, the fiestas are held in honor of a saint of the Roman Catholic Church. Fiestas are held throughout the year, and they vary from region to region. The fiesta of Corpus Christi, however, is celebrated in every region of Spain, at the end of May. This festival is a time for Roman Catholics to think about Jesus Christ and the importance of their religious faith.

Each region of Spain has its own special fiesta costume, decorated with embroidery or lace. Among the most beautiful of the fiesta costumes are those worn in Valencia. Women wear ornate combs in their hair. Their exquisite silk dresses are trimmed with rich Valencian lace.

Ferias, or fairs, often accompany or follow the religious festivals. *Feria de abril* ("April Fair"), which follows *Semana Santa* ("Holy Week") in Seville, is among the most famous. It began as a horse-trading fair nearly 2,000 years ago. The *feria* includes parades of showhorses and displays of fireworks.

Festival-goers gather in flamenco costumes for a fiesta in Jerez de La Frontera, in Andalusia.

La Fiesta de Santiago

No saint is more honored in Spain than Santiago, one of Jesus Christ's twelve disciples, or followers. Santiago (in English, Saint James) is the patron saint of Spain.

Santiago became a symbol of Christianity in Spain. There were even reports of him appearing in battle against the Muslims on a white charger. A great cathedral was built in Galicia on the site of Santiago's grave. His remains are kept in the crypt, a special vault under the altar. Santiago de Compostela, the town where the cathedral is located, is one of the great pilgrimage sites in all of Christianity.

41

Horseback riders, buggy rides, colorful lights, and decorations all add to the fun at Seville's Feria de abril.

Thousands travel to Santiago de Compostela every July for *La Fiesta de Santiago*. Crowds fill the plaza in front of the cathedral late on the night of July 24. A spectacular display of fireworks marks the beginning of the festivities. Cardboard, Muslim-style arches set up before the cathedral doors are burned down to remember Christianity's victory over Islam in Spain. On July 25, Santiago's feast day, a religious service is held in the cathedral. Afterward, there are parades with huge papier-mâché figures and much celebration with food and wine.

Lent and Holy Week

For two days before the long period of fasting and penance known as Lent, the people joyously celebrate another fiesta: *Carnaval* ("Carnival"). A famous *carnaval* is held every year in Andalusia's port city of Cádiz.

As Easter approaches, Christians begin preparations for *Semana Santa*, or Holy Week. At this solemn time, Catholics observe the Passion of Christ, the events leading up to Jesus Christ's crucifixion.

The most dramatic *Semana Santa* activities occur in Andalusia's capital, Seville. For seven evenings—and at dawn on Good Friday—leading up to Easter Sunday, people join solemn processions. They dress in black and speak only in whispers. These activities center around Seville's ancient cathedral, one of the largest Christian churches in the world.

Many of the men of Seville belong to one of more than sixty *cofradías*, or "brotherhoods." These religious associations may date as far back as the 1300s. The members of each *cofradía* build one or more *pasos*, or platforms. Each *paso* represents a scene from the Passion of Christ. During the processions, the *pasos* are carried by *cofradía* members, dressed somberly in hoods and cloaks.

A Christmas Season

Christmas, like Easter, is a very special time in Spain. The *belen*, or nativity scene, showing the birth of Jesus Christ, is often the center of the Christmas celebration in the home. Each day, miniature Three Kings are inched closer to the tiny manger. Families and friends exchange gifts, often placed in willow baskets, throughout the last two weeks of December. *La cena de nochebuena*—Christmas Eve dinner—is a time for family members to celebrate together. The main course is usually a roast turkey. Everyone attends midnight mass—a service at the local church—and then joins friends in the streets, singing carols (*villancicos*), dancing, and sampling more food.

The traditional family gift exchange in Spain occurs not on Christmas Day but on January 6. This day, called the Feast of the Epiphany, observes the visit of the Three Kings to the Infant Jesus. The day is often marked by camels passing through the streets, mounted by men costumed as the Three Kings. People also celebrate the Epiphany by eating *roscon*, or Twelfth Night cake.

A Valencian Treat

The *Fallas de San José* is one of the liveliest of all of Spain's festivals. It occurs every March in Valencia. San José, or Saint Joseph, is the patron saint of carpenters. What began as a good time by carpenters with their leftover wood scraps has evolved into a major festival.

A great deal of time and money goes into making *fallas*, huge papier-mâché figures that are carried through the streets of Valencia during the week. Many of the *fallas* make fun of public figures or national and international events. At midnight on the last day of the fiesta, Valencians gather to watch the burning of the *fallas*.

The Sound of Hooves Approaching

There are many festivals in Spain that involve running with the bulls. The most famous is *Fiesta de San Fermín*, which takes place in July in the city of Pamplona, in the Navarre region. San Fermín is the patron saint of bullfighters.

Imagine that you are one of thousands in the narrow streets of Pamplona about to take part in the *encierro*, the running of the bulls. In this ancient event, six bulls race through the narrow streets in the heart of the city. Their destination is the bullfighting arena.

44

Young men prove their courage as they "run with the bulls" during the traditional Pamplona festival.

At 8:00 A.M., a rocket explodes in the sky. This is the signal that the bulls have been released from their pens, and the race begins. Your heart begins pounding as you hear shouting. You know that the bulls are approaching.

Now everyone around you is running. You turn and run, too. People are pushing to get out of the way. You know that you cannot outrun the huge, powerful animals that are thundering toward you. You can only hope that they will pass by and not run over you! You notice that the more experienced participants are not looking back as they run. Frightened people jump up onto the pavement.

Then the bulls thunder past you. Soon a final rocket signals that the bulls have entered the bullring. In two minutes, the annual race is complete.

You have run with the bulls. For the rest of the festival, you will be telling people of your experience, and they will listen to you with respect. Now you truly know Spain.

Dressing in costumes for the Fiesta of San Juan is part of the fun of growing up in Alicante, in the Valencia region of Spain.

4

SCHOOL AND RECREATION

A Passion for
Learning and Play

In School...

For centuries, Spain's educational system did not benefit all people in the country. That has changed dramatically in recent decades. Today, education is required for all children between the ages of six and fourteen. It is free, paid for by the state.

Because of Spain's tradition of the siesta—the long rest period in the middle of the day—school may last until early evening. In past years, Spanish children attended school on Saturdays. That is no longer the case at most schools.

Regional governments are responsible for watching over the educational systems in their areas. As a result, children who live in the Galician, Basque, or Catalonian regions are required to study their regional language.

In *primaria*, or primary school, children study such subjects as science, math, and Spanish. Then they must pass a test before moving into *secundaria*, or secondary school. Students begin secondary school at age fourteen and attend for three years. A fourth year is required for those going on to the university, which many more young people are able to do today. A major test is held at the end of the fourth year. Those students who do not pass the test must repeat the entire year of school.

Children who choose not to attend secondary school must instead attend a vocational school for two years. There, they learn a trade, such as working with tools to make machines. If they wish, they can then continue their training for two more years to learn even more specialized skills in their trade.

. . . and Out

Fútbol—known in the United States as soccer—is a passion in Spain. Many children begin to develop their *fútbol* skills almost from the time they learn to walk.

Bicycling is another very popular sport, second only to soccer. One of the greatest professional cyclists in the world is the Spaniard Miguel Indurain. He won the Tour de France, the world's most important bicycle race, for five years in a row. In 1996, Indurain also represented his country in the Summer Olympic Games.

Another favorite sport is *pelota* (the Spanish word for "ball"). This sport originated in the Basque region. Although there are many variations, the basic game of *pelota* involves hitting a ball off a wall to an opponent. Today, children playing *pelota* against the side of a white-painted building is a very common sight in Spain.

Pelota is not only strenuous but also fast-paced. As a result, it is well suited as a spectator sport. The most popular modern version of the game involves a *chistera*, a special, curved glove with a wooden frame. This version of *pelota*, called jai alai (HI-lie), is played professionally in many places around the world.

Long, thin branches serve as hockey sticks for this group of Catalan boys.

Beach, Fun, and Mountains

Much of Spain's border is coastline. The beaches along the coast of the Mediterranean Sea are particularly lovely. The sands are crowded during the summer, especially in August, with people who love Spain's seashore.

In addition to swimming and water skiing, windsurfing is very popular in Spain. Beaches west of Gibraltar are especially good for this water sport. Windsurfers from all over the world travel to this region in search of thrills atop the Atlantic waves.

Such warm-weather sports as golf and tennis have also gained large followings in recent years. The Spaniards Seve

Spaniards love the sunny beaches and mild waters of the Mediterranean Sea.

Ballesteros and José Maria Olazábal are among the world's greatest golfers. Maria Casals and Manuel Santana made news as accomplished tennis players. Today, Barcelona's Arantxa Sánchez Vicario is one of the top tennis players in the world.

Spain's many mountains offer lots of opportunities for recreation. Many Spaniards enjoy hiking and mountain climbing in the summer and skiing in the winter. Ski resorts in the Pyrenees and Cantabrian Mountains are popular.

Los Toros

The entire arena is packed with thousands of spectators. There is great excitement in the air. The people are about to witness a *corrida de toro*, a "bullfight."

The bullfight begins at 5:00 P.M. sharp with the playing of a trumpet. A procession of men enters the arena. Some are on horses. Others are on foot. These are the *toreros*, the professional bullfighters. Each of the different types of *toreros* has a specific task and can be identified by his costume. The costumes, some of which were designed in the 1600s, are colorful and form-fitting. In the end, the bullfight comes down to the *matador de toro*—the "bull-killer"—facing the bull alone in the center of the arena.

Bullfighting's beginnings have been traced back to ancient times in Andalusia. By the 1700s, it was an important part of the culture of Spain. For centuries, bulls have been bred specifically for bullfighting. The practice seems cruel and offensive to many foreign visitors, but Spanish fans consider bullfighting an art.

Today, many of the smaller towns of Spain have a *plaza de toros*, or arena, for bullfighting. The major cities have arenas that can hold 20,000 people or more!

A bullfight in Madrid draws thousands of spectators.

Flamenco dancing is a spirited tradition in southern Spain, accompanied by dramatic guitar music and castanets. The ruffled dresses worn by these young women enhance their artistic movements.

5
THE ARTS

Reflecting a
Rich History

Music and Dance for All Ages

With their rich history, it is no surprise that Spaniards have an equally rich culture. This culture is woven into their daily lives most clearly in music and dance.

These arts take many forms in Spain. They have always been very important for children.

In days past, children often performed traditional songs and dances. In "The Tip and Heel Dance," for example, boys and girls would form a circle and dance in rhythm to the music as they sang.

Another favorite was "I Have a Little Doll." Girls would point to a doll's clothing as they sang about it.

Spain also has a great tradition of folk songs. Some of them, like "La Tarara," are still quite popular. "La Tarara" can often be heard at mountain picnics, on the beach, and even along city streets.

Soulful Music and Dance

Today, flamenco music and dance are enjoyed throughout Spain. Flamenco *is* Spain. When you see the young woman move to the guitarist's music, you can feel the romance of Spain. Flamenco music is intended to reflect the harshness of life. The sad *cante jondo*, or "deep song," accompanies the rhythmic beat. Yet underneath the somber mood of the flamenco is a passion that reflects the Spanish people's joyous zest for life.

In flamenco dance, toe and heel clicking is combined with both smooth and sharp body movements. These movements are punctuated by the clicking of castanets—small wooden clappers—and the enthusiastic shouts of ¡*Ole!* ("Bravo!") from the crowd.

Flamenco music and dance began long ago with the Gypsies of the region of Andalusia. In fact, the guitar, which leads the dancers, was originally an Andalusian and Gypsy instrument. In the 1920s, a Spanish musician set out to earn respect for the traditional Spanish guitar, the six-stringed *vihuela* (vee-WAY-lah). This musician, Andrés Segovia, became renowned as the finest classical guitarist in the world.

As with everything else in Spain, the types of music that you hear or play, and the kinds of dance that you watch or perform, represent the different regions of the nation. For example, the Celtic influence in Galicia is reflected in *gaita* (GUY-tuh), or bagpipe, music. Meanwhile, the people of Catalonia very much like choral music—sung in the Catalan language, of course. In addition, the traditional regional dance called the *sardana* is commonly performed by Spaniards throughout Catalonia.

Friends and strangers alike join hands to dance the traditional sardana *in Barcelona, the capital of Catalonia.*

A Disappearing World

Spain has been known for its arts and crafts for centuries. When the Arabs controlled the Iberian Peninsula, they introduced many fine artistic techniques.

The textile industry was important in Arab Spain. Many of the techniques and designs that the Arabs brought to Spain from North Africa were unknown in Europe. The silkworm was introduced to Spain, as was the cultivation of flax.

55

GREAT SPANISH ARTISTS

Diego Velázquez (1599–1660) was one of the greatest artists in history. Born in Seville, he became the court painter for King Philip IV. His paintings include royal portraits as well as religious subjects. One of Velázquez's most famous paintings is *The Maids of Honour*.

Francisco de Goya (1746–1828) was also a court painter. Among his great masterpieces are *The Naked Maja* and *The Clothed Maja*, which he painted in 1800–1805. In 1808, while Goya was at the height of his career, Napoleon Bonaparte of France invaded Spain. In his paintings and etchings, Goya showed the tragedy and horrors of the resulting war.

Pablo Picasso (1881–1973) is considered by many people to be the greatest artist of the twentieth century. Picasso was among those who developed Cubism in the 1920s. This stark style of painting rejected traditional techniques and emphasized the flat, two-dimensional surface of the canvas. His most famous work, *Guernica*, was painted to show the horrors of the Spanish Civil War.

Salvador Dali (1904–1989), an eccentric and colorful artist from Catalonia, was one of the founders of surrealist painting. Surrealism is a style that blends dream and fantasy with the real world. Dali's paintings look strange and unnatural, but they are fascinating.

Salvador Dali's Swans Reflecting Elephants *has a strange, dreamlike quality.*

Beautiful silks and linens and embroidered designs were created in the cultured urban centers. Elaborate ironwork gratings over windows and metal latticework were also gifts of Arab Spain.

In recent times, homespun linen has disappeared for the most part. Flax is grown now in only a few places, having been replaced by more profitable crops. Beautiful fabrics can still be found in homes across Spain, stored in chests as family heirlooms. But, where a loom was once a part of every household, this is no longer the case. And many daughters leave their homes to live in the cities, where they do not expect to follow their mothers' and grandmothers' craft.

Traditions of Design

A rich tradition of needlework remains for those who still practice the craft. Certain needlework designs are unique to Spain, combining the Muslim Arab and Christian influences. These include religious designs, such as those symbolizing the Passion of Christ, and geometric designs from the Arab culture. Certain regions, such as Toledo, are well known for their embroidery. Tourists like to purchase the beautifully embroidered coverlets, table linens, doilies, and handkerchiefs.

Lace was once a thriving industry in Spain. The craft survives today in only a few places. Barcelona is one of a few such centers. In some rural areas, grandmothers still teach their granddaughters how to make lace. Today it is used mostly to decorate special folk costumes.

Basket weaving is an ancient craft. Years ago, craftspeople along the Mediterranean and Atlantic coasts wove baskets for fisherfolk. These days, baskets come in many different weaves, shapes, and sizes. In Andalusia, the baskets are generally woven from olive and willow branches. The Balearic Islanders work with palmetto, while Basques use chestnut and hazelnut. Branches are also woven into floor mats, traditional hats for farm workers, and even shoes!

Pottery has been an important craft in Spain for centuries, and it still thrives today. Each region has its own distinctive designs and glazes. Pieces in copper and bronze, introduced long ago by the Arabs, are also much loved.

In a shop in Toledo, a needleworker plys her craft. Around her are many examples of the kind of work that Spanish artisans have been creating for centuries.

MAN OF LETTERS, MAN OF COURAGE

During the Spanish Civil War and then later under the dictatorship of Francisco Franco, hundreds of thousands of Spaniards were killed. Among the most famous victims was the poet and playwright Federico García Lorca (1898–1936). He lost his life in the earliest days of the Civil War, at age thirty-eight. García Lorca's death became a symbol of the suffering of the people under a dictatorship.

García Lorca was a native of Andalusia. He studied at the University of Madrid. Among his friends was the famous surrealist painter Salvador Dali. García Lorca's first successful play was performed in 1927, and Dali designed the scenery for the stage. García Lorca's poetry became widely known throughout Spain during his first two years in Madrid, even before any of his poems were published. *The Gypsy Ballads*, published in 1928, was a great success and made him world-famous.

García Lorca wrote about love, compassion for the poor, cruelty, and violence. His works were banned in Spain under Franco. Today, however, his poetry is widely read and his plays are performed.

It is not surprising that leatherwork became a specialized craft in a nation that has had a tradition of livestock raising. The center of this trade is in Córdoba. The handcrafting of ornate leather bridles and harnesses is still a popular art form. Leather crafters today also make beautiful belts and purses.

Spain has changed in many ways during this century. Its rich past, however, endures in Spain's intricate crafts, music and dance, and other arts. In the future, the Spaniards' creativity and love of beauty will continue to bear fruit for all the world to enjoy.

Country Facts

Official Name: España (Spain)

Capital: Madrid

Location: in the extreme southwest of the European continent. The northern tip of Africa lies just across the Strait of Gibraltar.

Area: 194,898 square miles (504,784 square kilometers)

Elevation: *Highest:* Teide Peak, on the island of Tenerife, in the Canary Islands, 12,198 feet (3,718 meters); on the Spanish mainland, Mulhacen, 11,411 feet (3,478 meters). *Lowest:* sea level at coasts

Climate: hot summers; mild and rainy winters along the coast, but very cold inland

Population: 40,092,000. *Distribution:* 79 percent urban; 21 percent rural

Form of Government: constitutional monarchy

Important Products: *Natural Resources:* coal, iron ore, mercury, gypsum, zinc, lead, copper, cork, hydroelectric power. *Agriculture:* fruits, olives, vegetables, grains, fish, animal herding. *Industries:* textiles and clothing, footwear, food and beverages, metal manufacturing, chemicals, shipbuilding, auto manufacturing, tourism

Basic Unit of Money: peseta; 1 peseta = 100 céntimos

Languages: four officially recognized: Spanish, Catalan, Galician, and Euskera

Religion: 98 percent Roman Catholic

Flag: three horizontal bands: red (top), yellow (center) with the national coat of arms, and red (bottom)

National Anthem: *Marcha Royal* ("Royal March"); also known as the *Marcha Grenaderos* ("March of the Grenadiers")

Major Holidays: New Year's Day, January 1; Epiphany, January 6; St. Joseph, March 19; Easter, spring; Labor Day, May 1; Corpus

Christi, June 25; St. James, July 25; Assumption, August 15; Columbus Day, October 12; All Saints Day, November 1; Constitution Day, December 6; Immaculate Conception, December 8; Christmas, December 25

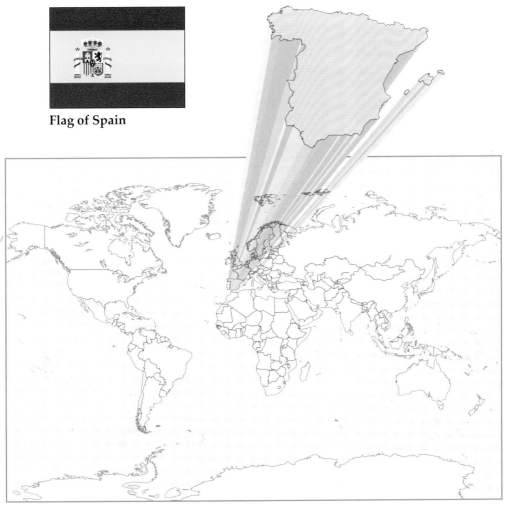

Flag of Spain

Spain in the World

Glossary

conquistadores (con-keys-tah-DOOR-ez): the "conquerors"; Spanish leaders who conquered many of the peoples of Latin America during the sixteenth century

Cortes: the Spanish Parliament, made up of a Congress and a Senate

dictatorship: a form of government in which all power is held by one person

Euskera (ay-oo-SKEH-rah): the native language of the people in the Basque region

flamenco: a lively dance performed to guitar music and castanet rhythm; the music itself

Inquisition: a time of religious intolerance and persecution in Spain, which began in 1478 and lasted until the early 1800s

Muslim: a follower of the religion of Islam. A Muslim believes that there is one God, Allah, and that Muhammad is his prophet. Most Arabs are Muslims.

mantilla (man-TEE-ya): a light scarf worn by Spanish women that covers the head and shoulders

Reconquista (ray-con-KEY-sta): the "Reconquering" of Spain; a time in which the Christian kingdoms of Spain banded together to defeat and drive out the Muslim Arabs

siesta: an afternoon nap or rest

tapas: small snacks eaten in the afternoon and early evening

For Further Reading

Cross, Esther and Cross, Wilbur. *Enchantment of the World, Spain.* Chicago: Childrens Press, 1985.

Epton, Nina. *Spanish Fiestas.* New York: A.S. Barnes and Company, 1968.

Kane, Robert. *Spain at Its Best.* Champlain, NY: Passport Books, 1988.

Kohen, Elizabeth. *Spain.* Tarrytown, NY: Marshall Cavendish, 1993.

Koslow, Philip. *El Cid.* New York: Chelsea Publishers, 1993.

Seth, Ronald. *Let's Visit Spain.* New York: Burke Publishing, 1984.

Spain in Pictures. Minneapolis, MN: Lerner Publication Company. 1995.

Index

Page numbers for illustrations are in boldface

About the Author

Stephen Chicoine was born and raised in Decatur, Illinois. He has an undergraduate degree in geology from the University of Illinois and a graduate degree in engineering and business from Stanford University.

He has traveled extensively in Spain and throughout Europe and also the more remote parts of the world.

Mr. Chicoine has written or supplied photographs for several nonfiction books for children and young adults. He lives in Houston, Texas, with his wife, Mary Ann, and their daughter, Maddie. His son, Jason, attends college in Vermont.